SHY GUIDES

THAT'S AWKWARD!

The Shy Guide to Embarrassing Situations

by Megan Cooley Peterson

Consultant:
Christopher A. Flessner, Ph.D.
Associate Professor, Department of Psychological Sciences
Director, Pediatric Anxiety Research Clinic (PARC)
Kent State University
Kent, Ohio

COMPASS POINT BOOKS
a capstone imprint

Compass Point Books are published by Capstone
1710 Roe Crest Drive, North Mankato, Minnesota 56003
www.mycapstone.com

Library of Congress Cataloging-in-Publication Data
Names: Peterson, Megan Cooley, author. Title: That's awkward!
: the shy guide to embarrassing situations / by Megan Cooley
Peterson. Description: North Mankato, Minnesota : Compass
Point Books, [2019] | Series: Shy guides | Audience: Age: 9-13. |
Audience: Grade 4 to 6. | Includes bibliographical references and
index. Identifiers: LCCN 2018045937| ISBN 9780756560201 (library
binding) | ISBN 9780756560249 (pbk.) | ISBN 9780756560287 (ebook
pdf) Subjects: LCSH: Bashfulness in children—Juvenile literature. |
Children—Life skills guides. Classification: LCC BF723.B3 P48 2019
| DDC 646.70083/4—dc23 LC record available at https://lccn.loc.
gov/2018045937

Editorial Credits
Abby Colich, editor; Kay Fraser, designer;
Morgan Walters, media researcher; Laura Manthe, production
specialist

Image Credits
Shutterstock: Africa Studio, 6, Andrea Raffin, 5, Daniel M Ernst,
31, Dave Clark Digital Photo, top 19, Diego Cervo, 8, Dragana
Jokmanovic, bottom 37, Featureflash Photo Agency, 45, Flamingo
Images, 11, 44, HstrongART, 25, Iakov Filimonov, 41, La Vieja Sirena,
39, LightField Studios, 28, MANDY GODBEHEAR, top 37, Mark
Nazh, Cover, 1, Monkey Business Images, 3, 21, 32, 35, Nejron
Photo, 20, nelen, 38, oneinchpunch, 17, panitanphoto, 23, Piyato,
9, Rawpixel.com, 15, 27, 33, Rohappy, 13, s_bukley, bottom 19, 29,
Shanti Hesse, 24, SpeedKingz, 7, 43, William Perugini, 16

TABLE OF CONTENTS

CHAPTER 1
THE TRUTH ABOUT FEELING AWKWARD

>>>>>>>>

Actress Jennifer Lawrence shot to fame in the blockbuster movies *The Hunger Games* and *X-Men*. She also became well known for her many awkward moments—in public! Lawrence has tripped on the red carpet at movie premieres and awards shows. She even fell on stage while accepting the Oscar for Best Actress!

How does Lawrence navigate awkward situations? With humor! When she fell at the Oscars, Lawrence picked herself back up, collected her trophy, and made a joke to the audience. Backstage, reporters wanted to talk about her fall more than her award. Lawrence poked fun at them—and at herself. She turned her stumble into one of the most charming moments in Academy Awards history.

Can you think of an awkward moment you had recently? Everyone, from movie stars to athletes, feels awkward and embarrassed from time to time. If you're someone who is considered shy or quiet, these awkward moments can be especially difficult. Learning more about these situations and more about yourself can help make them a little more tolerable.

AWKWARD OR EMBARRASSING?

What is the difference between an awkward situation and an embarrassing moment? Aren't they the same thing? Not quite.

Any situation that draws attention to you when you don't want it or aren't ready for it can cause an awkward moment. An awkward situation involves a social setting, such as school or the store. When something uncomfortable happens, such as a fall, people don't know what to do or say. The person at the center of the awkward moment might turn red or start to sweat. The people watching might look away or laugh nervously. Why? Because often they feel awkward on behalf of another person. This is called empathy. Empathy is the ability to understand how someone else is feeling and imagine how they feel.

Embarrassment is more personal than just feeling awkward. An embarrassed person believes that he or she has done something wrong. They might experience shame or guilt. For example, if someone answers a question incorrectly in class, he or she might feel embarrassed. Feeling awkward or embarrassed are closely related. They are often experienced at the same time.

A GOOD THING

Think about all the groups you belong to—your family, your classmates, your friends. Being part of a group makes us feel safe. Everyone feels embarrassed in these groups at one time or another. Feeling embarrassed in these groups may actually be a good thing sometimes.

The feeling that you've "messed up" may let you know when you've made a social mistake. If you've done something wrong, feeling embarrassed about it also shows others in the group that you're sorry for the slip-up.

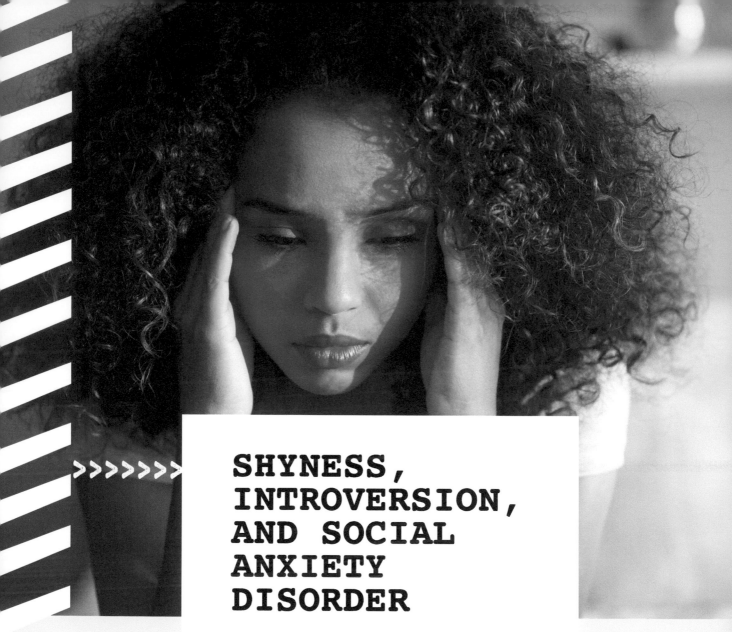

SHYNESS, INTROVERSION, AND SOCIAL ANXIETY DISORDER

Awkward situations and embarrassing moments can be even more uncomfortable for people who are shy or have social anxiety. Understanding the differences among shyness, introversion, and social anxiety will help you better understand yourself and how to deal with these situations.

Shy people have a fear of being judged in social situations. They might be outgoing at home or with friends, but they tend to close themselves off in social situations. The more nervous a person feels, the more likely he or she is to experience an awkward situation.

Shyness is not the same thing as introversion. Introverts feel more comfortable in quieter, low-key environments. They don't crave social settings the way extroverts do. A shy person can be an extrovert, and an outgoing person can be an introvert. But usually, shy people are also introverts.

Social anxiety disorder goes beyond just feeling nervous or shy around other people. People with social anxiety disorder may experience anxiety in a variety of social situations. They may experience fear asking questions in class, starting a conversation with someone they don't know well, standing up for themselves, or participating in extracurricular activities. They are afraid that people are watching or judging them. An everyday situation, such as being called on in class, can cause extreme stress for people with social anxiety.

Try not to worry too much about whether you're introverted or shy. You may even be a little of both. And that's OK. If you have the right tools, you can help ease any awkward situation.

>> IS BEING SHY A BAD THING?

Extroverts and bold personality types often get more attention. It may seem like it's "better" to be more talkative or outgoing. Does that mean shy people should try to change their personalities to become more outgoing? Absolutely not! You should never feel pressured to change yourself. Most people aren't just shy or outgoing, introverted or extroverted. A person may have a little of each trait.

LIFE TIP

If you think you might have social anxiety disorder or another mental health issue, talk to a parent or another trusted adult. They can help you get professional help. You can also use the resources on page 46.

It's easy to imagine that outgoing people never feel awkward. That's not true. Everyone experiences awkward or embarrassing moments. What's awkward or embarrassing for one person might not be for someone else. Also people react differently to awkward situations. A really outgoing person just might not show that he or she feels embarrassed. Or he or she might show it differently.

Take the following quiz to see how you would handle these potentially cringe-worthy moments. See how your reactions compare to those of others.

>>>>>> QUIZ: HOW DO YOU DEAL WITH AWKWARD SITUATIONS?

1. You're in a large crowd at a local street festival. Someone bumps into you. You accidentally spill a smoothie down the front of your shirt. Would you...
   a) Run all the way to the parking lot and hide until your dad comes to pick you up?
   b) Freeze in shock, but then let your friends help you get cleaned up?
   c) Laugh about it. Then try to win a clean T-shirt at the next game?

2. Your best friend takes you to a birthday party where you don't know anyone. He disappears to talk to someone else. Would you...
   a) Find a couch and sit down by yourself until your friend is ready to leave?
   b) Walk around, hoping someone will strike up a conversation?
   c) Grab a piece of birthday cake and start a game of Twister with the first person you meet?

3. Your mom drops you off at school and yells, "Have a good day, munchkin!" in front of other students. Some of them laugh. Would you...
   a) Cover your bright-red face and race past the other students?
   b) Ignore your mom and the laughing kids?
   c) Wave goodbye to your mom and not make a big deal out of it?

4. You run into someone you've met before but can't remember his name. He remembers yours. Would you...
   a) Make an excuse to leave as quickly as possible?
   b) Say, "Hey, you!" and pretend you know his name?
   c) Admit you forgot his name?

5. Your friend has a booger hanging out of her nose in math class. Would you...
   a) Avoid eye contact and hope someone else will tell her?
   b) Keep wiping your own nose, hoping she'll get the hint?
   c) Pull her aside and hand her a facial tissue?

HOW DID YOU ANSWER?

Mostly A's: You're an avoider. When it comes to awkward situations, you prefer to hide until the situation has passed.

Mostly B's: You tend to fake it until you make it. You're not super uncomfortable in awkward situations, but you're not quite sure how to handle them either.

Mostly C's: You go with the flow. You know everyone gets embarrassed, so why hide it? You use humor and honesty to get through awkward situations as quickly and as painlessly as possible.

No matter how you answered, learning more about awkward moments and how to handle them will help you feel more at ease in any social setting.

CHAPTER 2
FINDING
THE RIGHT TOOLS

Imagine you're going to help your neighbors build a skateboard ramp. You show up, but no one has a plan or any tools. So much for the ramp, right? The same is true when dealing with awkward situations. When you're equipped with the right tools, you'll be better able to handle awkward and embarrassing moments.

THE SPOTLIGHT EFFECT

Imagine walking into the school lunchroom, tripping over your untied shoelaces, and dropping your tray. Pieces of food spray in all directions. Your face gets hot, and your heart thumps wildly. So far, no one has noticed. Then a classmate approaches you. He asks if you're okay. He helps you clean up your tray and invites you to sit with him and his friends. You've just narrowly avoided a very awkward situation. Or have you?

In 2000 psychologists asked a group of college students to wear embarrassingly bright yellow T-shirts. The students went to class. After class, students guessed that half their classmates noticed their T-shirts. But the truth is that only about 25 percent of their classmates said they noticed the brightly colored shirts.

Psychologists named the students' reaction the spotlight effect. This is the tendency to think more people notice you than actually do. In embarrassing situations, you might feel like there's a "spotlight" on you. In reality, less people notice you than you think. That's one thing to keep in mind the next time you're feeling embarrassed.

POSITIVE VS. NEGATIVE SELF-TALK

When you feel awkward and embarrassed, what kinds of thoughts run through your mind? Do you beat yourself up? Do you call yourself names? Or do you remind yourself that you're human, and it's okay to make mistakes? Take the quiz below to see if you're a positive or a negative self-talker.

>>>>> QUIZ: HOW DO YOU TALK TO YOURSELF?

1. You're in the cafeteria and accidentally knock your milk onto your friend's brand-new jeans. You think to yourself...
   a) I hope my friend is okay! I better grab a towel and help her clean up.
   b) That was pretty clumsy of me.
   c) I am such a bad friend. I should probably find a new lunch table.

2. You're giving a speech in class when you accidentally belch. You think to yourself...
   a) I'm only human, and burping is natural.
   b) How embarrassing. I hope no one heard that!
   c) I am disgusting and will probably fail my speech.

3. Your math teacher asks you to come up to the front of the class and solve a problem. You get stuck halfway through. You think to yourself...
   a) I need to ask for help.
   b) Oh, geez. I completely forgot how to solve this problem!
   c) I am so stupid for not understanding this problem. I'm sure the rest of the class understands it.

LIFE TIP

Tape up some positive self-talk on your bedroom walls. Seeing it will help you remember to use it.

4. You wear a new outfit to school. As you walk down the hallway, you think to yourself...
   a) I can't wait to show my friends my new threads!
   b) I hope at least one person compliments me on my new outfit.
   c) People are staring at me. I must look ridiculous. I have the worst taste in fashion.

5. You try out for a sports team but don't make it. You think to yourself...
   a) I'm still glad I tried. I'll practice more for the next tryout.
   b) I'm really bummed I didn't make it. Now everyone will know.
   c) I can't believe I actually thought I could make the team. Of course I didn't get chosen.

HOW DID YOU ANSWER?

Mostly A's: You use mostly positive self-talk. You don't often drag yourself down. Good work! Keep up the positive self-talk.

Mostly B's: You use a mixture of both positive and negative self-talk. While you sometimes judge yourself a little too harshly, you try to stay positive as much as you can.

Mostly C's: You use mostly negative self-talk. You hold yourself to impossibly high standards.

If you answered mostly B's or C's, you have room for improvement. Carry a notebook for a day or two. Jot down your negative self-talk. Do you notice any patterns? Try to replace your negative messages with more positive messages. Try not to tell yourself, "I really messed up this time! I'm such a screw-up." Replace the negative self-talk with, "That was an interesting experience! I'll learn from it and do better next time."

CONFRONTING
YOUR EMBARRASSMENT

When facing a perceived threat, such as a situation you know will be awkward, your body has a physical reaction. You might breathe heavily. Your heart may pound. Your body is preparing you to either face the danger or to run away. This reaction is called the fight-or-flight response.

In 2012 researchers concluded that there are only two ways of dealing with embarrassing and awkward moments. A person can either pretend it didn't happen or confront the moment head-on. If you try to ignore what happened, the moment doesn't disappear. It lingers in the memories of those who witnessed it. The moment remains unresolved, which might actually make the awkward situation last longer.

So how do you face the situation? Researchers found that one of the best ways is to use humor. Let's say you're at a backyard birthday party. You accidentally fall into the pool with your clothes on. Everyone gasps. Instead of getting out and running away, you climb out of the pool, smile, and take a bow. By using humor, you let everyone know that you're not bothered by what happened. You also have resolved the situation in your mind. You change into some dry clothes, go on with your day. You don't think about the event anymore. If you had run away, you might still be left wondering what people thought.

>> How to Recover from an Awkward Situation

The most awkward situation of your life just happened. How can you recover?

1. Forgive yourself. Beating yourself up won't make you feel any better. Be your own best friend.

2. Distract yourself. Watch a movie or exercise. Listen to your favorite music. Bake a cake or make a pizza.

3. Think about what went right, not only on what went wrong. What can you learn?

4. Share what happened with a close friend or family member. Get his or her perspective.

5. Remember that everyone experiences awkward and embarrassing situations from time to time. It's a part of life!

CHAPTER 3
SWEATING THE SMALL STUFF

>>>>>>>

Toilet paper stuck to your shoe. Walking around with your pants zipper unzipped. A piece of spinach wedged between your two front teeth. Everyone has experienced these awkward moments. You've probably even been told a time or two not to "sweat the small stuff." Some awkward situations are definitely more serious. But sometimes it's the "small stuff" that makes you want to change your name and move to another school! Learning how to recognize and deal with some common smaller awkward moments will help you get through them with more confidence.

BATHROOM BLUNDERS

Hitting the bathroom is a pretty routine part of life. You use the toilet, shower, and brush your teeth every day. Some studies estimate that we spend 1.5 years of our *lives* in the bathroom. So we should be totally comfortable with whatever happens in there, right?

We all have awkward bathroom situations we wish we could flush down the toilet. If you're in a public restroom and run out of toilet paper, it can be mortifying to ask a stranger for some. Someone walking into the bathroom while you're on the toilet can be embarrassing. And what if your awkward situation goes beyond borrowing toilet paper? What if you flood the toilet at someone else's house or at school?

Some awkward bathroom moments, such as flooding a toilet, can't be avoided. Instead of running away, use humor to admit what happened. If you flooded the toilet, first find someone who can help you clean it up. Then make a joke about testing the limits of the plumbing. If someone accidentally walks into your stall, smile and wave. You'll be surprised by how many people can relate to what you're going through. Everyone uses the bathroom, and people will soon forget what happened. You should too.

LIFE TIP

If you're feeling awkward about a bathroom blunder, imagine your favorite celebrity sitting on the toilet. It might make you laugh and help you relax.

>> Lady Gaga Keeps It Real

Singer-songwriter Lady Gaga gives new meaning to the saying, "When you've gotta go, you've gotta go!" While on tour, Gaga's dressing rooms don't always have bathrooms. If she has to pee between costume changes, she goes in a trash can! She says peeing in the garbage sometimes makes more sense than walking down the hall naked to use the bathroom. Others might think peeing in anything other than a toilet would be embarrassing. But Lady Gaga isn't afraid to talk about it. She isn't worried about what others think. Taking this approach can help you too.

19

EATING IN PUBLIC

Eating in public is another pretty common experience, until something goes wrong. Then it becomes stressful, especially when it feels like all eyes are on you. You can take some steps to avoid feeling awkward at the table before you even take your first bite. Avoid that messy order of barbeque ribs or spaghetti. Stick to simpler, easier-to-eat meals. Take small bites. Smaller bites are easier to chew. You'll be less likely to spill on yourself. Keep a napkin close by, just in case you have a spill or need to wipe your mouth.

MEALTIME MISHAPS

Everyone's been there. A piece of food gets stuck in your teeth, or you spill food all over yourself. You might wonder how many people noticed that bit of broccoli camped out in your smile or the stain on your shirt. Use humor to diffuse the awkward moment before it starts. For example, say, "I guess my shirt *doesn't* make a very good napkin!" When you finally notice the food in your teeth, say, "I was keeping it as a snack for later!"

Sometimes you won't realize you've had a mealtime mishap until someone else points it out. If this happens, try not to panic. The person isn't trying to embarrass you. He or she is trying to help you avoid an awkward situation. Thank the person for their honesty and move on. You can make jokes, too, if it helps calm you.

Remember this if *you* notice someone else spilled or has food in their teeth. Instead of pretending the food isn't there, pull your friend aside. Tell him or her quietly. Your friend will be far less embarrassed than if you announce it to the entire lunch table. The moment will end almost before it started.

LIFE TIP

Try an experiment—walk around the mall with a splat of ketchup on your shirt. The longer you walk around, the less awkward you'll feel. Living in the moment shows you that you can get through awkward situations.

CHAPTER 4
SCHOOL
SLIP-UPS

School is packed with possibilities for awkward situations, from changing before gym class to passing gas in front of your classmates. It is possible to deal with most of the embarrassing and awkward moments that might crop up after the first bell rings. Here are some common awkward moments and how to come out the other side unscathed.

AND THE ANSWER IS...

Everyone daydreams from time to time, even in school. But what happens if your teacher calls on you in the middle of a daydreaming session? Resist the urge to lie. Be honest and admit that you didn't hear the question. Apologize for not paying attention. Lying only makes the situation worse—and might even get you into trouble. If your teacher repeats the question and you don't know the answer, admit that as well. You're in school for a reason—to learn. Learning means you won't have all the answers, and that's okay!

IS THIS THE RIGHT ROOM?

You slip into class just as the bell rings and sit at your desk. Then you look up. An unfamiliar teacher stands at the front of the class. And your best friend who usually sits right next to you has been replaced by someone else. Then the truth hits—you've just gone into the wrong classroom!

This minor mishap will only turn into a huge, embarrassing moment if *you* let it. Find the humor in the moment. Stand up and say, "I thought I'd try a different class today, but I think I'll stick with my old one." Then hustle to the correct classroom. If you can laugh at yourself, the awkward feeling will fade more quickly.

LOCKER ROOM BLUES

It's normal to want privacy when changing your clothes. But in the locker room, privacy is almost impossible. Since the invention of the locker room itself, people have found it awkward to change in front of others. Some people change underneath a large T-shirt or even hide in a bathroom stall to get changed.

So what do you do when it feels like everyone's staring at you in your underwear? It might help to know that most of your classmates feel just as awkward. In fact, if you looked around the locker room, you'd probably see that most people keep their heads down as they change.

Your body might be going through a lot of changes. That can affect the way you view yourself. A positive body image will make changing in the locker room feel less awkward. Use positive self-talk to remind yourself of reasons to love your body. Focus less on how your body *looks* and more on *what* it can do. Maybe you love to dance or can dunk a basketball. Perhaps you're a budding chef or an expert gamer. When you think of all the amazing things your body can do, you'll feel less awkward changing in front of other people.

If you have a negative image of your body, you're not alone. Most people have a part of their body they want to change. The entertainment industry often portrays a certain body type as ideal. If you find yourself getting down about your body, take a break from media. Get outside for a walk or a bike ride. Plant a garden or organize a scavenger hunt with your friends. You might find focusing on activities you enjoy helps you bounce back from negative feelings about your body.

>> Retouched Images

You see endless images of people every day in advertisements. Almost all of these images have been retouched or altered. It can be hard to see these images and not feel like you need to look the same. But it's important to realize that many of these images aren't real. Several companies have even stopped using retouched photos in their ads. These companies know that altered images can harm young people's self-image.

AWKWARD GROUP PROJECTS

Group projects are a great way to learn how to work with other people. But working with your classmates can be awkward, especially if you're shy.

Group projects tend to go well if the members are comfortable with one another. Get to know the other group members a little first. Talk about your favorite TV shows or sports teams. After your group breaks the ice, everyone will be more comfortable digging into the project. If you feel awkward sharing your ideas, write them down first. Then share them with the group.

PUBLIC SPEAKING FLUBS

Giving a speech in class feels awkward for a lot of people. Imagine you flub your words or forget what you were going to say. Maybe you're too quiet and the teacher asks you to speak up. Maybe you drop your note cards, and your hands shake so badly you can't put them back into the correct order.

If this happens, pause for a moment. Take a deep breath and smile. This will help you relax. You can even say, "Please excuse me. I'm so nervous." People appreciate honesty. And being honest might make you feel better. You might even notice someone in the audience smiling or nodding in agreement.

You can also use positive self-talk in this situation. Say to yourself, "Most people are nervous talking in front of others." Or, "I have done this before. It was just fine even though I was nervous." Giving yourself a little pep talk may make you feel better.

Practice talking in front of an audience. This will help you feel more confident and less awkward. Start out with just a couple people. Make a silly speech in front of your family or friends. As you gain confidence, stretch your limits. Act out your favorite movie scene with a friend in the cafeteria. If other people stop and stare, keep going. You might feel awkward at first, but that feeling will fade. Once you get more comfortable with social attention, public speaking will seem less scary.

FACING PUBLIC
REJECTION

Running for student council or trying out for a team can be a lot of fun. It can also be scary. Giving a speech or playing a sport with everyone watching can make you nervous. You might be afraid to even try. You might be fearful of what could happen if you don't make the team or get elected.

Public rejection can feel like a giant arrow is pointing directly at you. If someone asks you about it, be honest. Pretending the rejection is not a big deal won't make you feel any better. Let yourself be sad if you need to be, but don't let yourself dwell on it for too long. You might also feel a little jealous of those who made the team, especially if your friends got picked and you didn't. It's completely normal to feel that way, but don't let it get in the way of your friendship. Remind yourself that being rejected doesn't mean you're a failure. All successful people are rejected sometimes. The only people who never face rejection are those who are too afraid to try at all.

After a few days, think about your tryout, audition, or election. Write down what went well and what you could have done better. Ask your coach or teacher for tips on how to improve. You can also look for other activities that interest you.

COMFORTING A FRIEND

Now imagine the roles are reversed—you made the team, but your friend didn't. It may feel awkward to talk about it with your friend. But avoiding the topic will only make your friend feel worse. Ignoring a friend's disappointment might hurt their feelings more than you realize.

Have empathy for your friend's pain. Tell him you're sorry he didn't make it. Let him know you're always there for him if he needs to talk.

>> Carmelo Anthony

Carmelo Anthony is a star forward for the Houston Rockets. But back in high school, he didn't make the basketball team! Anthony's coach thought he was too short. He cut him from the team. Anthony's rejection pushed him to work even harder.

CHAPTER 5

BEING THE NEW GUY OR GIRL

Everyone will be the new person at school, in a club, or on a team at some point in their lives. The unknown can be terrifying. What if you have trouble making new friends? What if you have to eat lunch alone? What if you get lost in your new school?

Being the new person can be scary when you don't know anyone. But you *do* know yourself. Don't try to reinvent who you are in your new school, club, or team. Trying to invent a new personality will only make you feel more awkward around new people. Being true to who you are is your biggest asset. Use it.

STARTING A NEW SCHOOL

Starting a new school is tough for everyone, especially for shy people. As you walk down the hallway, it might feel like everyone's staring at you. How can you make that first day feel less awkward?

Visit your new school before your first day. If it's possible, see if a parent or guardian can set up a special tour on the weekend. Find your locker and classrooms. You won't have to worry about getting lost on your first day.

Keep your expectations low. If you worry that you'll have an awkward first day, chances are you probably will. It's all about expectations. If you go into your first day with an open mind, you might be surprised by how smoothly it goes.

Dress for comfort—and confidence. Do you have a special outfit that gives you confidence? Wear it! If you're unsure, try on a few outfits. See what makes you feel comfortable. Don't try to wear a trendy new outfit to fit in. It will only make you feel more self-conscious.

Ask questions. Can't find your math class? Forgot to bring a pencil? Don't know where the bathroom is? Ask for help if you need it. Everyone needs help from time to time. Asking for help might even help you make a new friend.

JOINING A NEW GROUP

You've just joined a new team. At your first practice, your coach makes you stand in front of your teammates. She asks you to say a few words about yourself. You don't know what to say. When practice starts, you knock over some equipment. Then you botch every play you try to make. Should you quit the team?

Not so fast! Joining a new team or group can be intimidating, especially if your new teammates have been playing together for a long time. You can't expect yourself to walk in on the first day and fit right in. Being nervous can make you more distracted and prone to mistakes. It takes time and patience to fit in with a new team or group.

The good news about your new team or club is that you're surrounded by people who share a similar passion. Whether you've joined the school play or the chess club, you're already more bonded with your fellow group members than you realize. Strike up a conversation with them about favorite music or movies or sports players. People love to talk about things they enjoy.

>> Body Language and Confidence

Do you slouch or avoid eye contact in social situations? Research shows that your body language affects your confidence. Crossing your arms over your chest and looking down can actually make you feel less powerful. Changing your posture or the way you walk can change the way you feel about yourself in social situations. Sit up straight. Straighten your posture when you walk. Keep your head up. Make eye contact when speaking to someone. If you find this difficult to do, try practicing at home with a parent or friend before trying it in public. You might discover that using confident body language helps you feel less awkward.

Be Yourself

MAKING A NEW FRIEND

Chances are your friendships are one of the most important parts of your life. Friends listen when you're feeling down. They go on adventures with you and laugh at your jokes. They warn you when you're about to make a mistake. Researchers say friendships are important to overall happiness. It's not surprising, then, that making new friends can be intimidating. You may fear that someone will judge you or fear that you will be rejected. How can you get past your own awkwardness?

Find common interests. Trying to strike up a friendship with someone you have nothing in common with or have just met can get awkward quickly. Approach people you share an interest with, such as a teammate or someone you've joked with in class.

Start out slow. Say hi to someone in the hallway or after practice. At lunch, ask the person if you can sit at his or her table. Show interest in their conversations, and join in when you can. It will probably feel awkward, and that's normal. Eventually the awkward feeling will pass.

Ask questions. Asking questions will help you feel less awkward when getting to know someone new. Ask a potential new friend about their interests and future plans. Showing interest in someone else is a great way to ease any awkward moment. It also shows you care.

CHAPTER 6

WHEN THINGS GET WEIRD WITH FRIENDS

Awkward situations don't just happen when you join a new group or give a speech at school. They even happen with the people who know you best—your friends.

WHEN A NEW FRIEND REJECTS YOU

Once you become more comfortable with a possible new friend, you might decide to ask him or her to hang out. All great friendships have to start somewhere, but it can still be terrifying to put yourself out there. You might fear they will reject you.

In this situation, remember that making a new friend is a numbers game. There are billions of people on Earth, each with their own distinct personality. Not every personality is going to click with yours. If someone turns down your invite, tell them you understand. Don't take it personally. Afterward, you might feel sad. Allow yourself to do that. Talk to a parent or trusted adult about what happened. They've likely experienced something similar and can relate to what you're going through. Tell yourself that this was just one incident. Remind yourself of your positive qualities and all the reasons you're a good friend.

The next time you see that person, be friendly. Avoiding him or her will make things more awkward. Once time passes, you won't feel so bad about the rejection. Then you can put more energy into connecting with other people.

LIFE TIP

Being turned down by a potential new friend might actually be a blessing in disguise. A rejection means it probably wasn't a good match. Now you can focus on possible friends who are better suited to you.

>> Letting Go of Perfectionism

The pressure to be liked by everyone can drive some people toward perfectionism. One reason people try to be "perfect" is really the need to control how others view you. Constantly worrying about what others think of you can make you feel like a puppet on a string, constantly performing. Perfection is a myth. No matter how hard you try, not everyone is going to have a positive opinion of you. Instead of trying to be perfect, focus on what makes you feel good about yourself. Once you stop trying to be perfect, awkward situations might not feel as earth-shattering as they once did. Don't waste your energy trying to impress people. A true friend will like you for who you are.

DISAGREEMENTS WITH FRIENDS

You probably feel like you're usually in sync with your friends. But when you disagree with a friend, it can feel painfully awkward. Perhaps you found a favorite new band and your friend makes fun of it. Disagreeing with a friend can feel so awkward you might be tempted to avoid the situation altogether.

No two people are going to agree on everything, all the time. So what happens when you disagree? Be respectful. Tell your friend that you disagree and explain why. Focus on how you feel first instead of focusing on what he said or did. For example, say, "I feel upset because you…" Don't start off by saying, "You did this, and I'm really upset!" Your friend might get defensive and refuse to listen. Agree with your friend that it's okay to disagree on a topic and still remain friends.

Imagine your best friend can't make it to your birthday party. You get upset at her. You shoot off an angry text message to another friend about her. You feel better—until your phone chirps. You receive a message back from your best friend. You accidentally sent the angry message to her! You want to crawl into bed and hide under the covers.

You know you just wanted to vent and get your anger off your chest. But you ended up hurting your best friend's feelings in the process. It can be embarrassing to hurt someone's feelings. If that happens, the best thing to do is to own up to your mistake right away. Apologize and ask what you can do to make things better.

ENDING A FRIENDSHIP

Sometimes friendships run their course. People sometimes naturally grow apart. Other times, a friendship may make you feel unhappy or unsafe. It may be time to end it. Ending a friendship can be extremely awkward. You don't want to hurt anyone's feelings. But it's kinder to be honest than to just disappear from someone's life with no explanation.

To end a friendship, speak to your friend face-to-face. First, thank her for her friendship. Then explain that you're not happy. Say you think it's best to part ways. Your friend might get angry or sad, and that's okay. She has the right to feel how she feels. After you've ended the friendship, you'll likely feel like a weight has been lifted from your shoulders. If not, give it some time. Allow yourself to feel a little sad that the friendship is over. Focus on making plans with other friends or making new ones.

When you see your former friend at school or a party, it will likely feel awkward. Don't ignore her or treat her in a disrespectful way. Be kind and say hello. If the other person isn't ready to speak yet, give her space. As time passes, the hurt feelings will ease. In the long run, your old friend will be glad you cared enough to be honest.

LIFE TIP

If your friend suddenly has no time for you or continually cancels plans, ask him what's going on. If he can't or won't be honest, it might be best to leave him alone for a while. Trying to force someone to spend time with you will only make you feel bad. It also won't work. Focus on your other friendships.

CHAPTER 7
TEASING AND BULLYING

Everyone gets teased at some point. Maybe you spilled on your T-shirt and someone makes a silly comment about it. Teasing may seem harmless, but it can be awkward for the person being teased. If you're being teased, use humor to shrug it off. Smile and say, "You got me!" If the teasing hurts your feelings, say so. The teaser might not be aware of how his words make you feel.

HOW TEASING AND BULLYING DIFFER

The words teasing and bullying mean different things. Bullying might start out as teasing. If you try to laugh off the teasing and the person still won't leave you alone, you're dealing with a bully. A bully is not trying to be silly or get a laugh. Bullies try to hurt others on purpose with words or violence. Spreading rumors, making fun of someone over and over, or threatening to hit someone are all ways of bullying.

HOW TO DEAL WITH BULLYING

Dealing with a bully isn't easy, but there are a few things you can do. First, try not to react. Walk away if you can. A bully wants to see you get upset or angry. If you don't react, the bully may lose interest and leave you alone. Try to surround yourself with friends. That might make it more difficult for the bully to get close to you. If the bully still won't leave you alone, tell a parent or teacher. Your school likely has an anti-bullying policy and should enforce it.

If you see someone being bullied, try to help the victim. Invite the victim to sit with you at lunch or walk with you down the hallway. Your presence will make the victim feel safer and might make the bully leave. Also, get an adult to help. Standing up for what is right might be difficult, but you'll feel proud that you took action.

>> Why Do People Bully?

Psychologists study why some children bully others. Research has shown that children who are abused at home are more likely to become bullies. A bully's parents might ignore him or her at home or use physical punishments. Many bullies don't feel good about themselves. They act out and pick on others to make themselves feel more important.

LIFE TIP

Take a break from social media if you're being cyberbullied. Log out of all your accounts, and focus on things you enjoy doing. Read a book outside or organize a game night with friends.

CYBERBULLYING

If you're being bullied online, never respond to the bully. They want you to reply, which will only make them bully you more. Tell a parent or trusted adult right away, and keep a record of any threatening e-mails or posts. Block the person or account that's bullying you. If things get worse, your parent can help you contact your internet provider or the police.

>> Taylor Swift

Music superstar Taylor Swift was bullied in junior high. When she would sit down in the lunchroom, her classmates would move away from her. Starting at age 12, Swift channeled her feelings into songwriting. She wrote about the pain caused by bullying in her songs.

THAT'S AWKWARD, BUT YOU'RE NOT ALONE!

You can't avoid awkward and embarrassing situations entirely. They happen to everyone. Even celebrities are photographed tripping on the red carpet or smiling with a piece of food stuck in their teeth! Learning how to navigate awkward moments will make them easier to deal with in the future.

ASK FOR HELP

If you believe you're suffering from anxiety, depression, or another mental health issue or are the victim of bullying, ask for help. Reach out to a teacher, school counselor, parent, or another trusted adult. Doctors, psychologists, and social workers are available to get you the help you need. You can also reach out to one of these organizations below.

National Safe Place
provides immediate help and safety to any youth in crisis
https://www.nationalsafeplace.org/
Text SAFE and your current location to 4HELP (44357) for immediate help.

National Suicide Prevention
national network of local crisis centers that provide free and confidential
    support
https://suicidepreventionlifeline.org/
800-273-8255

Stomp Out Bullying!
national nonprofit dedicated to preventing bullying, cyberbullying, and other
    digital abuse
http://stompoutbullying.org/

Teen Line
teen-to-teen hotline for when you just need someone to talk to
https://teenlineonline.org/
310-855-4673
Text TEEN to 839863.

Trevor Project
leading national organization providing crisis intervention and suicide
    prevention services to LGBTQ youth
https://www.thetrevorproject.org
866-488-7386
Text START to 678678.

READ MORE

Andrus, Aubre. *Stress Less: How to Achieve Inner Calm and Relaxation.* Stress-Busting Survival Guides. North Mankato, Minn.: Capstone Press, 2018.

Cain, Susan. *Quiet Power: The Secret Strengths of Introverts.* New York: Dial Books for Young Readers, 2016.

Jacobsen, Aryelle. *A Is for Awkward: A Guide to Surviving Middle School.* Asheville, N.C.: InnerQuest, 2017.

Poole, H.W. *Social Fears.* Childhood Fears and Anxieties. Broomall, Pcnn.: Mason Crest, 2018.

INTERNET SITES

Use FactHound to find Internet sites related to this book.

Visit *www.facthound.com*

Just type in 9780756560201 and go.

 **Super-cool stuff!** Check out projects, games and lots more at **www.capstonekids.com**

INDEX